EASY UKULELE

A Complete, Quick and Easy Beginner Ukulele Method for Kids and Adults

PIERRE HACHÉ MUSIC

Author: Pierre Haché
Editor: Heather Jamieson
Interior and Cover Design: Eoin Hickey
ISBN: 9781086376821
Copyright © 2019 Pierre Haché
Revised 2021

pierrehachemusic.com

A heartfelt THANK YOU to everyone who was involved in the creation of this book, and to all my dedicated students who helped shape its contents.

Beginner Ukulele Videos

PIERRE HACHÉ MUSIC **YouTube**

Join the **Beginner Ukulele Videos** Facebook Group
and **SUBSCRIBE** to **Pierre Hache Music** on YouTube
for **FUN, FREE & EASY UKULELE VIDEOS** to complement this book!

*A little practice every day
Goes a long way!*

AUTHOR'S NOTE

Music can inspire, soothe and bring smiles to listeners and performers alike. These pages are designed to give novice musicians of any age the tools to begin strumming and singing as soon as possible, and to feel and share the joy of music.

The exercises and tips found herein stem from more than 15 years of experience teaching students of all ages. My most important advice is to work on one thing at a time; don't skip the basics; practice a little almost every day; and SLOW DOWN! Speed will come. Consistency and patience is the key.

Note that the chord diagrams in this beginner ukulele method are oriented horizontally, like a ukulele on its side or being held in the playing position. I find it easier to teach beginners this way, as it matches the way you will be holding your instrument and the pictures in the book. However, keep in mind that chord diagrams are often shown as an upright ukulele, as if it's hanging on a wall.

I have published a companion book to *Easy Ukulele* which applies this tried and true approach to learning to play the guitar. *Easy Guitar* is also available on Amazon.

I've also created a YouTube channel, **Pierre Hache Music**, with tons of FREE ukulele and guitar videos to help you out along the way. It includes demonstrations of many of the songs found in this book! Feel free to look it up and subscribe to stay tuned.

Thanks and happy strumming!

Pierre

In this *Easy Ukulele* book you will learn basic exercises, chords and rhythms… and before you know it, you will be able to strum and sing 21 fun songs! Perfect for beginners of all ages, it is also a great tool for parents to teach their kids. This complete, clear and concise method will even prepare you to play your favorite pop songs! Progress through these pages at your own pace, and most of all, enjoy!

TABLE OF CONTENTS

1.	Song List	p.2
2.	A Note on Practice	p.3
3.	How to Hold your Ukulele	p.3
4.	Tuning and String Numbers - Part 1	p.4
5.	Tuning and String Numbers - Part 2	p.5
6.	Chords, Fingers and Frets	p.6
7.	Single Note Exercise	p.8
8.	C Major Scale	p.9
9.	Basic Strumming	p.10
10.	How to Practice Songs	p.11
11.	Songs	p.12
12.	Chord Progressions	p.24
13.	Strumming Patterns	p.25
14.	More Chords	p.26
15.	Pop Song Examples	p.27

1. SONG LIST

Hot Cross Buns **(C,G)**	p.12
Row Your Boat	p.12
The Wheels On The Bus	p.13
London Bridge **(F)**	p.14
You Are My Sunshine	p.14
If You're Happy	p.15
The Itsy Bitsy Spider **(Am)**	p.15
Rock-A-Bye Baby **(G7)**	p.16
Are You Sleeping?	p.16
Happy Birthday	p.17
Twinkle Twinkle / Alphabet Song	p.17
Yankee Doodle	p.18
This Old Man	p.18
Oh! Susanna	p.19
Baa Baa Black Sheep	p.19
Silent Night **(C7)**	p.20
Amazing Grace	p.20
She'll Be Coming **(D7)**	p.21
Love Me Do **(D)**	p.22
House Of The Rising Sun **(E7)**	p.22
Jingle Bells **(A7)**	p.23

EASY UKULELE

2. A NOTE ON PRACTICE

The key to learning any instrument is regular practice. Three times a week for five to 10 minutes is plenty to start. As you build up to 10 to 20 minutes, your progress will be much faster! Remember to have fun and work on one thing at a time, developing your skills step-by-step. It's also OK to skip ahead and try some songs right away!

3. HOW TO HOLD YOUR UKULELE

Let's dive right in! For right-handed players, hold the main body of the ukulele by pressing it against your body with your right forearm. Your fingers should be near the sound hole. This may be a little awkward at first, but the idea is to support and strum the instrument with your right arm, while the left holds up the neck and presses on the strings to change the notes. You can play either standing or sitting on a solid chair; always mindful of keeping your back straight. A music stand or something to hold your music near eye level will help with posture and concentration.

For left-handed players simply switch it around: hold the ukulele against your body with your left forearm, while the right hand supports the neck and presses the strings.

EASY UKULELE

4. TUNING AND STRING NUMBERS PART 1

Now that you know how to hold your instrument, an important first step to making your ukulele sound wonderful is to tune it. The easiest ways are to either use a tuner or a tuning app, or tune by ear with an instrument, video or app.

To tune with an electronic tuner, simply attach it to the head of the ukulele or hold it near the strings, and pluck one string at a time. Turn the connected peg until the tuner shows the desired note. Tightening the strings will raise the pitch, while loosening them will lower it.

The 4th string, or the one closest to your chin, should be a G. The 3rd string a C, the 2nd an E, and finally the 1st string (the one nearest your feet) should be an A.

A great phrase to remember the string names from top to bottom is **G**ood **C**hildren **E**at **A**pples. If tuning this way does the trick, then feel free to move on to trying some chords!

EASY UKULELE

5. TUNING AND STRING NUMBERS PART 2

You can also use another instrument (such as a piano) or any video or app that plays the desired notes.

Simply play a G on the instrument and match the pitch on your G string by turning the corresponding tuning peg. Or, listen to the video or app and match the pitches, making sure you're tuning the right string to the right note. Repeat the same process for the C, E and A strings. This method works best for someone with a good ear or some musical training.

EASY UKULELE

6. CHORDS, FINGERS AND FRETS ....

The next step is to learn some basic chords. You can try them all now or start with a few easy ones, such as C6, C and Am (A minor). The yellow numbers in the chord diagrams tell you which finger to use; 1 for index, 2 for middle finger, and so on. When pressing the strings, it is important to keep your thumb behind the neck and use the tips of your fingers to avoid touching or muting the adjacent strings. You should be pressing between the metal bars. Once in position, gently strum all the strings downwards with your other hand, either with your thumb, index finger or a pick. Choose whichever method feels most natural to you. Listen, be patient and adjust your position until all the notes ring clearly. It may take a few days to get the hang of the G chord so be patient! Regular practice is the key.

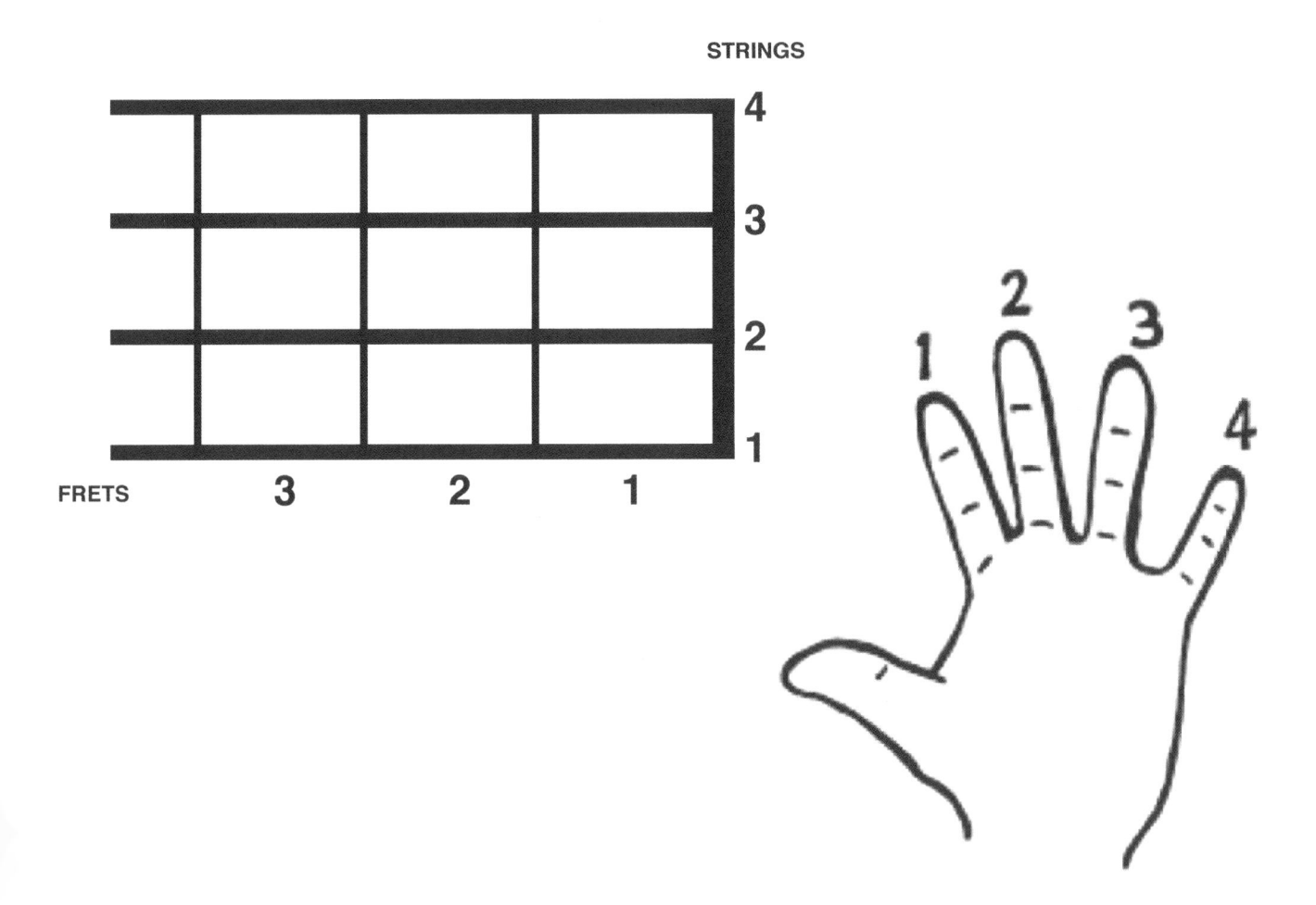

STRINGS

FRETS   3   2   1

EASY UKULELE

BASIC CHORDS

C6 - all open strings (no pressing)

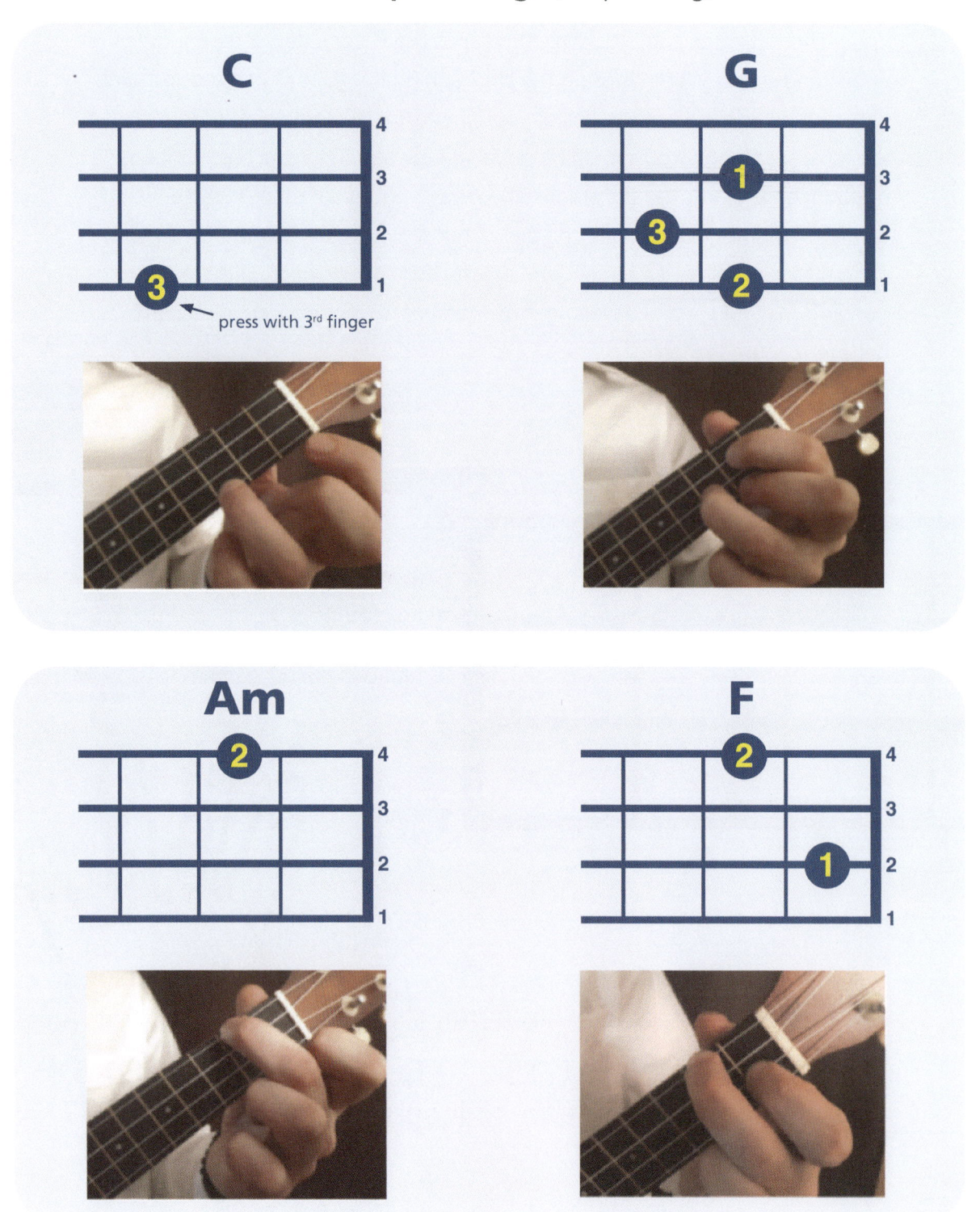

C
- 3rd finger: 1st fret (press with 3rd finger)

G
- 1: 2nd fret
- 3: 2nd fret
- 2: 3rd fret

Am
- 2: 2nd fret

F
- 2: 1st fret
- 1: 2nd fret

EASY UKULELE

7. SINGLE NOTE EXERCISE

Before moving on to strumming and songs, it helps to begin with a simple finger exercise. This exercise will develop your finger control and independence, as well as coordination between both hands. It is also a good first step towards playing some of the harder chords. Use it as a warm-up for your first few practice sessions.

To begin, simply press, or pinch the first fret of the first string with your first finger. Then pluck only that string. Listen for a clear ringing note. If it sounds more like a click or a buzzing sound, you may not be pressing on the right spot or firmly enough. Adjust your finger until the note rings clearly. Then slowly move on to the second fret with your second finger and pluck that note.

Continue with finger three on fret three and finger four on fret four.

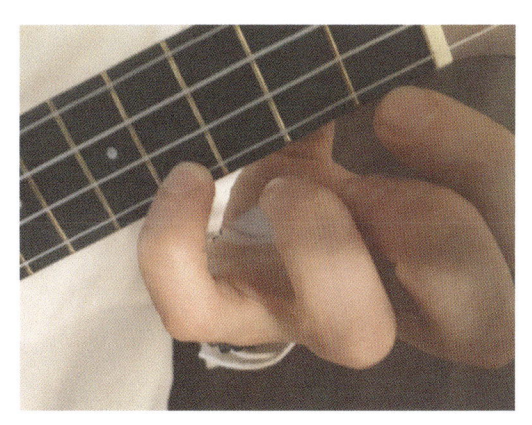

Repeat in the opposite direction, slowly pressing and plucking frets 4, 3, 2, and 1 with the respective finger.

Once you get the hang of this, try it on the other strings. You can also vary the order, such as 1, 3, 2, 4 or 4, 2, 1, 3.

EASY UKULELE

8. C MAJOR SCALE

To play a C major scale, start by plucking the C or 3rd string open (without pressing any frets). Then press the second fret on that string with your second finger and pluck it to play a D note. The next three notes (E, F and G) will be played on the E string: first open, then 1st fret and 3rd fret. The last 3 notes (A, B and C) are on the A string: open, 2nd fret and 3rd fret. See the diagram to help understand the sequence. Learn this eight note scale by heart and play it at a slow and steady pace. Try playing it in the reverse order as well. Feel free to hum along, eventually singing the note names.

C Major Scale

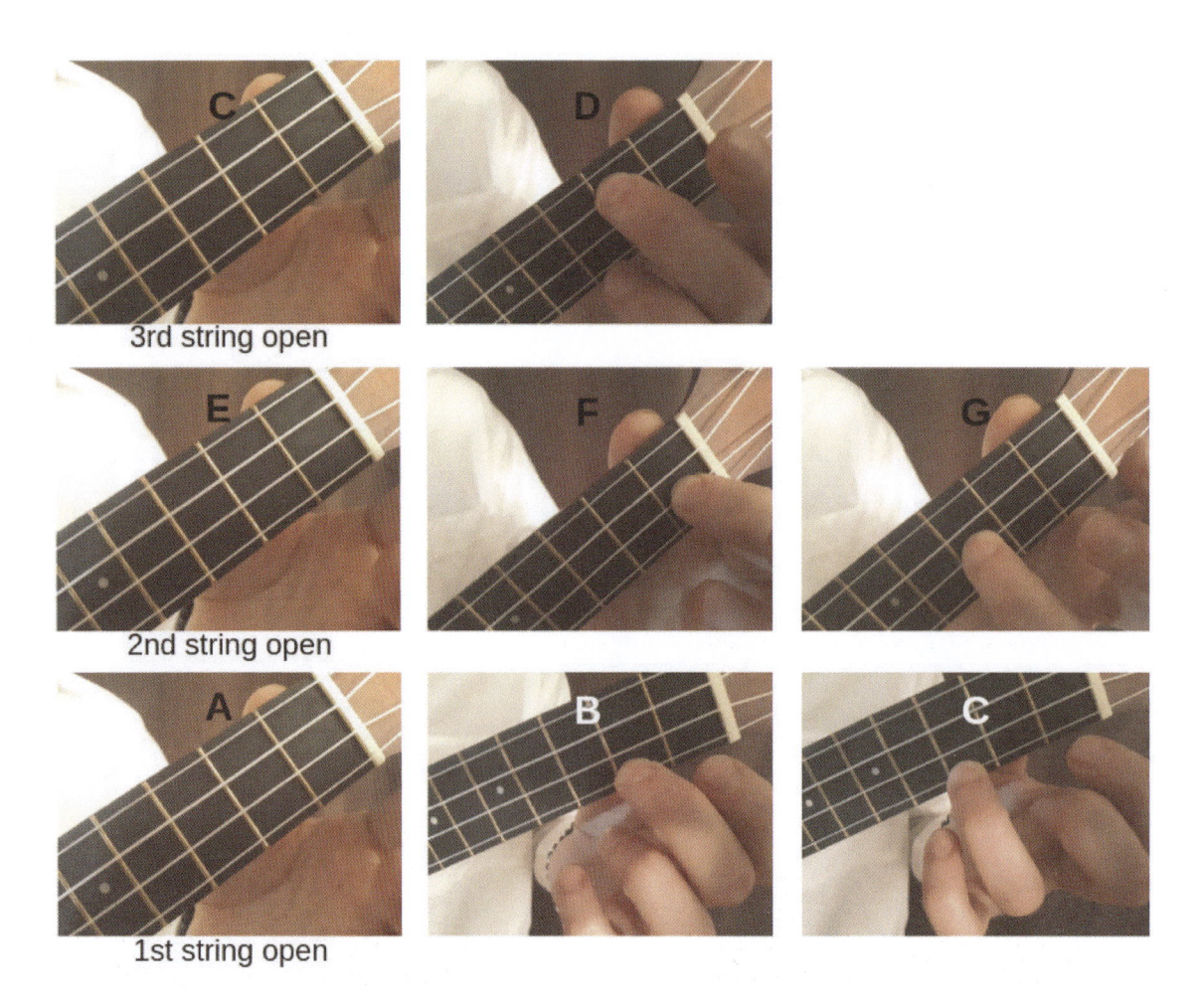

C	D
3rd string open	

E	F	G
2nd string open		

A	B	C
1st string open		

EASY UKULELE

9. BASIC STRUMMING

Begin by slowly counting out loud from one to four repeatedly: 1, 2, 3, 4, 1, 2, 3, 4 and so on. For the first rhythm, strum a chord, let's say C, as you say 1. Hold the chord so it rings while you count the rest of the beats. This step is very important as it will prepare you to strum and sing at the same time.

Once this feels comfortable, transition to another chord during beat 4 so that the next strum on 1 sounds different. Be careful to keep your count steady and start with easier chords, such as C6, C or Am. Later you can come back to work on the trickier chords like G and F.

For the second rhythm, strum only on beats 1 and 3, eventually transitioning to another chord during beat 4.

The third and final rhythm has you strumming on all 4 beats: 1, 2, 3, 4, 1, 2, 3, 4. Try to switch quickly, as you only have the time between beat 4 and beat 1 to get to the next chord. Go slow at first and keep your count steady.

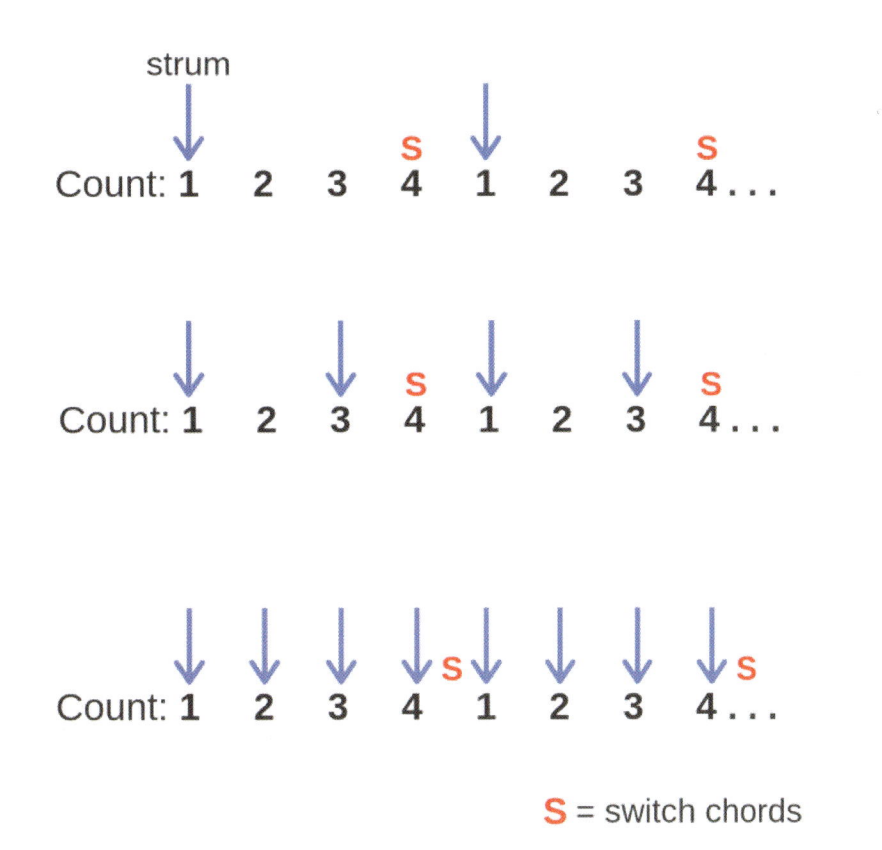

S = switch chords

10. HOW TO PRACTICE SONGS

Now that you know how to hold and tune your ukulele, as well as strum chords in time, you're ready to play some songs. We'll start with some familiar children's melodies: not only are they great for kids, their simplicity and familiarity also make them perfect learning tools for adults.

Beginners may want to spend a few days on each song, while students with some musical experience can move more quickly to the more advanced songs and pop progressions.

As an entry point to working on these songs, simply **sing the melody**. If there are any you aren't familiar with, do a quick YouTube search and listen to a couple of versions. Having the tune in mind will make your practice much more productive and musical!

Make sure you know how to play the chords in the song. Remember to keep your thumb behind the neck and press with the tips of your fingers to avoid muting any strings.

An excellent warm-up is to switch between the hardest chords of the song 10 to 20 times. Don't rush – aim for smooth and efficient movements. This step will really help with more challenging chords!

Next, strum through the chords of the song at a slow and steady pace **without singing.**

Now that you have the melody in mind, and are familiar with the chord progression, it's time to put the strumming and singing together! The chords have been carefully placed above the correct syllable to help with timing. Note that if a chord has no word below it, it is strummed without singing. Enjoy!

11. SONGS

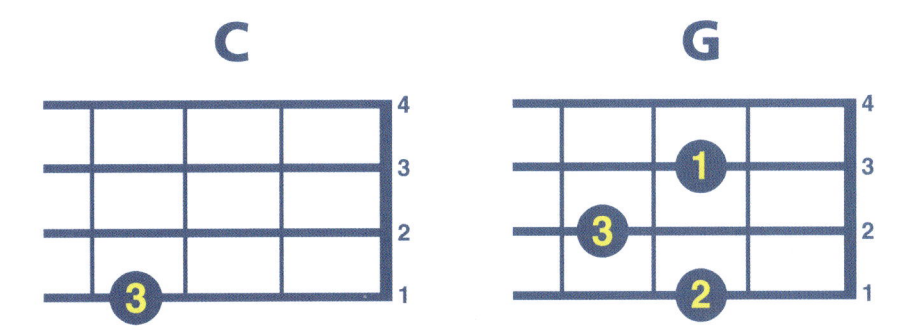

C **G**

HOT CROSS BUNS

C C C C C C

Hot cross buns, hot cross buns,

C   G

One a penny, two a penny,

C C C

Hot cross buns.

ROW YOUR BOAT

C   C   C   C

Row, row, row your boat,

C   C   C   C

Gently down the stream.

C   C   C   C

Merrily, merrily, merrily, merrily,

G   G   C

Life is but a dream.

EASY UKULELE

THE WHEELS ON THE BUS

       C   **C**   **C**   **C**
The wheels on the bus go round and round,

   G   **G**   **G**   **G**
Round and round, round and round,

       C   **C**   **C**   **C**
The wheels on the bus go round and round,

G G   **C C**
All through the town.

The wipers on the bus go swish, swish, swish…

The horn on the bus goes beep, beep, beep…

The doors on the bus go open and shut…

The driver on the bus goes "move on back"…

The babies on the bus go "wah, wah, wah"…

The mommies on the bus go "shush, shush, shush"

(All verses use the same 2 chords!)

Hope you're having fun! By the way, my YouTube channel, **Pierre Hache Music**, includes tons of free ukulele content to help you out! Consider subscribing to stay tuned! ;)

Also, if you're finding this book helpful, a positive review on **Amazon** goes a long way! Thanks in advance and happy strumming!

EASY UKULELE

F

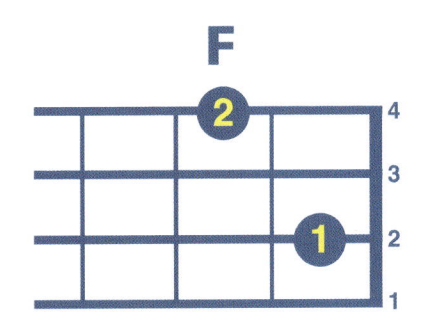

LONDON BRIDGE

     F   **F**   **F**   **F**
London Bridge is falling down,

  C   **C**   **F**   **F**
Falling down, falling down,

     F   **F**   **F**   **F**
London Bridge is falling down,

C C F
My fair lady.

YOU ARE MY SUNSHINE

       C **C** **C**   **C** **C** **C** **C**
You are my sunshine,   my only sunshine,

     C   **F** **F** **F**   **F** **C** **C** **C**
You make me happy,   when skies are grey.

     C   **F** **F** **F**   **F** **C** **C** **C**
You'll never know dear, how much I love you,

C   **C**   **G** **G** **C** **C**
Please don't take my sunshine away.

IF YOU'RE HAPPY AND YOU KNOW IT

        C   C   G   G
If you're happy and you know it clap your hands!

        G   G   C   C
If you're happy and you know it clap your hands!

        F   F
If you're happy and you know it,

        C   C
And you really want to show it.

        G   G   C
If you're happy and you know it clap your hands!

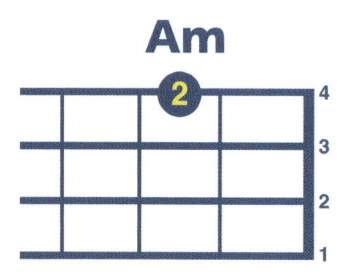

Am

THE ITSY BITSY SPIDER

      C   C   G   C
The itsy bitsy spider climbed up the water spout.

Am   **Am**   F   C
Down came the rain, and washed the spider out.

   C   C   G   C
Out came the sun and dried up all the rain

   C   C   G   C
And the itsy bitsy spider climbed up the spout again!

EASY UKULELE

NEW CHORD

G7

ROCK-A-BYE BABY

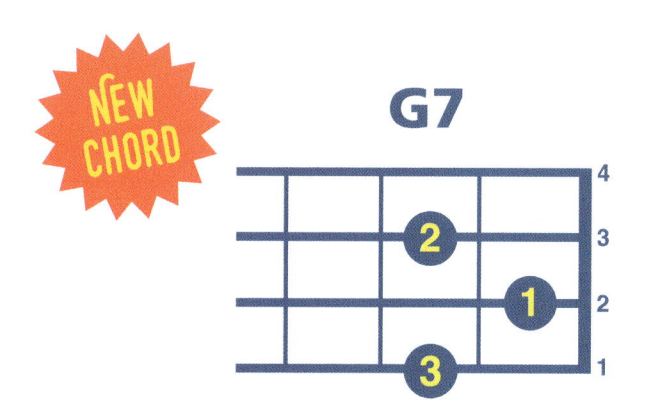

   C   C C   G7
Rock-a-bye baby on the tree top,

 G7   G7   G7   C
When the wind blows, the cradle will rock.

  C   C   C   G7
When the bough breaks, the cradle will fall,

 G7   C G7   C
And down will come baby, cradle and all.

ARE YOU SLEEPING?

  C   C   C   C
Are you sleeping? Are you sleeping?

C G7 C C G7 C
Brother John, Brother John.

  C   C   C   C
London bells are ringing, London bells are ringing.

C G7 C C G7 C
Ding, dang, dong. Ding dang dong!

EASY UKULELE

HAPPY BIRTHDAY

        C   **G7**
Happy birthday to you,

       G7   **C**
Happy birthday to you,

       C   **F**
Happy birthday, Happy birthday,

      G7   **C**
Happy birthday to you!

TWINKLE TWINKLE / ALPHABET SONG

    C   **C**   **F** **C**
Twinkle, twinkle little star,

F   **C**   **G7**   **C**
How I wonder what you are.

C **G7**   **C**   **G7**
Up above the world so high,

C   **G7** **C**   **G7**
Like a diamond in the sky.

    C   **C**   **F** **C**
Twinkle, twinkle little star,

F   **C**   **G7**   **C**
How I wonder what you are.

EASY UKULELE

YANKEE DOODLE

    C   C   C   G7   C   C   C G7
Yankee Doodle went to town, riding on a pony.

    C   C   F   F   G7   G7 C C
Stuck a feather in his cap, and called it macaroni!

THIS OLD MAN

   C   C   C   C
This old man, he played one,

   F   F   G7   G7
He played knick-knack on my thumb.

   C   C   C   C
Knick-knack paddy-whack, give a dog a bone.

   G7   G7   G7   C
This old man came rolling home.

Repeat same chords and lyrics with: *two, shoe*
                                                          three, knee
                                                          four, door
                                                          five, hive
                                                          six, sticks
                                                          seven, up in heaven
                                                          eight, gate
                                                          nine, spine
                                                          ten, once again!

OH! SUSANNA

     C   C C   C   C   C   G7 G7
I come from Alabama with a banjo on my knee.

     C   C   C   C   C   G7   C C
We're goin' to Louisiana, our true love for to see.

F F F   F   C C   G7 G7
Oh Susanna!   Oh don't you cry for me.

    C   C   C   C G7 C
We're goin' to Louisiana just to play ukulele!

BAA BAA BLACK SHEEP

 C   C   F   C
Baa, baa black sheep, have you any wool?

G7 C   G7   C
Yes sir, yes sir, three bags full.

 C   F C   G7
One for the master, one for the dame,

 C   F   C   G7
And one for the little boy who lives down the lane.

 C   C   F   C
Baa, baa black sheep, have you any wool?

G7 C   G7   C
Yes sir, yes sir, three bags full.

SILENT NIGHT

C C C C
Silent night, Holy night.

G G C C7
All is calm, all is bright.

F F C C
Round yon virgin, mother and child.

F F C C
Holy infant, so tender and mild.

G7 G7 C C
Sleep in heavenly peace oh,

C G7 C
Sleep in heavenly peace.

AMAZING GRACE

C C7 F C
Amazing Grace! How sweet the sound.

C C G7 G7
That saved a wretch like me!

C C7 F C
I once was lost, but now am found,

Am G7 F C
Was blind, but now I see.

NEW CHORD

D7

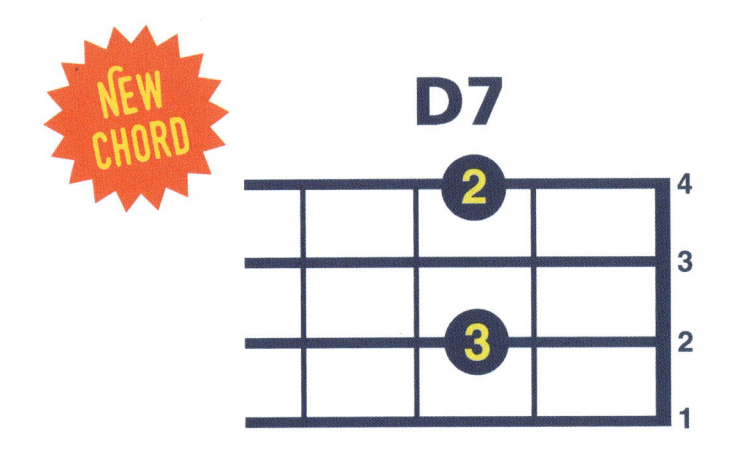

SHE'LL BE COMING

      C   **C**   **C**   **C**   **C**   **C**   **C**

She'll be coming round the mountain when she comes.

   C   **C**   **C**   **C**   **C**   **G7**   **G7**   **G7**

She'll be coming round the mountain when she comes.

G7   **C**   **C**   **C7**

She'll be coming round the mountain,

C7   **F**   **F**   **D7**

She'll be coming round the mountain,

D7   **C**   **C**   **G7**   **G7**   **C** **G7** **C**

She'll be coming round the mountain when she comes.

I've also created the **Easy Ukulele Online Course**, in which I explain, strum and sing every song and exercise from this book and more! With more than 20 lessons worth of material for the price of one, it is sure to take your learning to the next level. Check it out at **Pierrehachemusic.com**!

NEW CHORD

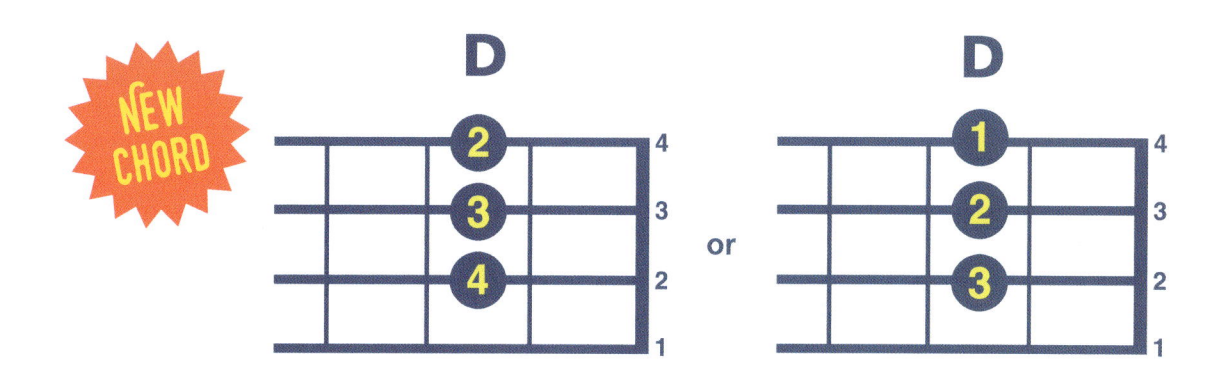

D or **D**

LOVE ME DO

G　　　　　C　　　G　　　　　　C
Love, love me do.　You know I love you.

G　　　　　　C　　　C　　C　　C
I'll always be true.　　So ple-e-e-ease,

G　　　C　　G　　　　　C
Love me do.　Whoa, love me do!

D　　　　　　D　　C　　　　G
Someone to love, somebody new.

D　　　　　　D　　C　　　　　G
Someone to love, someone like you!

HOUSE OF THE RISING SUN

Am　　C　　D　　　F
There is a house in New Orleans,

Am　　　C　　E7　　E7
They call the Rising Sun.

Am　　C　　D　　　　F
And it's been the ruin of many a poor boy.

Am　　E7　　Am
And God, I know I'm one.

NEW CHORD

E7

EASY UKULELE

JINGLE BELLS

   G   **G**
Dashing through the snow,

   G   **C**
In a one-horse open sleigh.

  Am   **D7**
Through the fields we go,

 D7   **G**
Laughing all the way.

  G   **G**
Bells on bob-tails ring,

  G   **C**
Making spirits bright.

  Am   **D**
What fun it is to ride and sing

 D7   **G**   **D7**
A sleighing song tonight. Oh!

NEW CHORD

A7

  G **G** **G**   **G**   **G** **C** **G** **G**
Jingle bells, jingle bells, jingle all the way!

C   **C**   **G** **G**   **A7**   **A7**   **D7** **D7**
Oh what fun it is to ride, in a one-horse open sleigh, Hey!

  G **G** **G**   **G**   **G** **C** **G** **G**
Jingle bells, jingle bells, jingle all the way!

C   **C**   **G** **G**   **D7**   **D7** **G**
Oh what fun it is to ride, in a one-horse open sleigh!

EASY UKULELE

12. CHORD PROGRESSIONS

Each of the following chord progressions can be found in a variety of pop and rock songs. If you can play these chords with a few of the rhythms provided in **Section 13,** you'll be more than ready to tackle your favorite songs. You'll be surprised how many songs you can play with the chords you already know! It's easy to look up the chords to your favorite songs and give them a try. Start with one strum per chord, then see which strumming pattern fits best.

1. G C G C
2. C G7 C G7
3. C C G7 C
4. D G D G
5. G G D7 G

6. G F C C
7. C F G7 G7
8. Am F C C
9. Am D7 G G
10. F C G7 C

11. G D G C
12. C G Am F
13. C Am F G
14. Am C G F
15. Am F C G

EASY UKULELE

13. STRUMMING PATTERNS

The following are eight common strumming patterns that fit with all the chord progressions from **Section 12**. Don't worry, there's no need to try all the combinations! Start by choosing a few chord progressions that sound good to you and are comfortable to play. Then, you can try one rhythm at a time. Just like in **Section 9**, it really helps to start by **counting out loud.** As with all the exercises in this book, start slowly. Eventually, these will sound great at a medium and fast pace. The arrows tell you in which direction to strum and the "M" means to mute, or gently slap the strings with the palm of your hand to stop the sound.

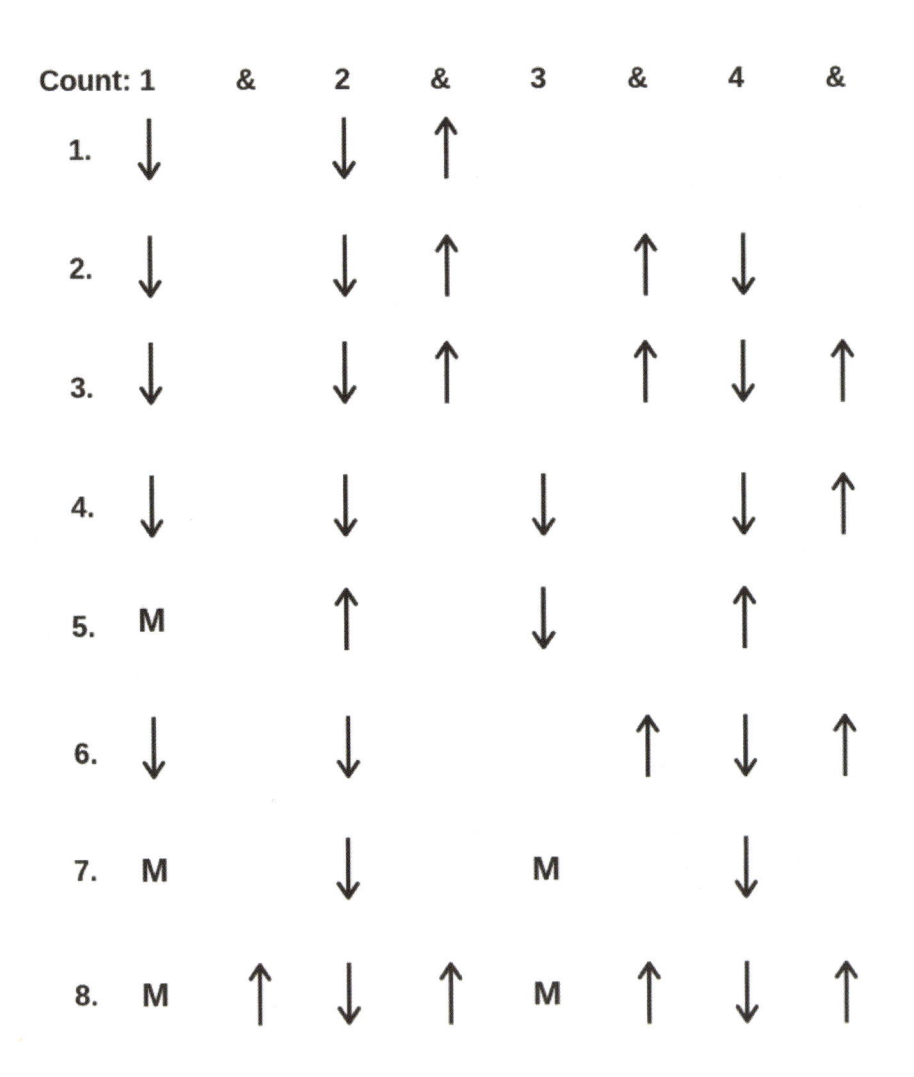

Count:	1	&	2	&	3	&	4	&
1.	↓		↓	↑				
2.	↓		↓	↑			↑	↓
3.	↓		↓	↑		↑	↓	↑
4.	↓		↓		↓		↓	↑
5.	M		↑		↓		↑	
6.	↓		↓			↑	↓	↑
7.	M		↓		M		↓	
8.	M	↑	↓	↑	M	↑	↓	↑

EASY UKULELE

14. MORE CHORDS

The following chart will help when you come across chords you don't know. (As in **Section 15.**) Chords with many "1"s will require you to bar, or press many strings with a flattened first finger. This may take some time to get used to. Keep in mind, any unlisted chord is a quick internet search away. Have fun building your repertoire of songs to strum, sing and share!

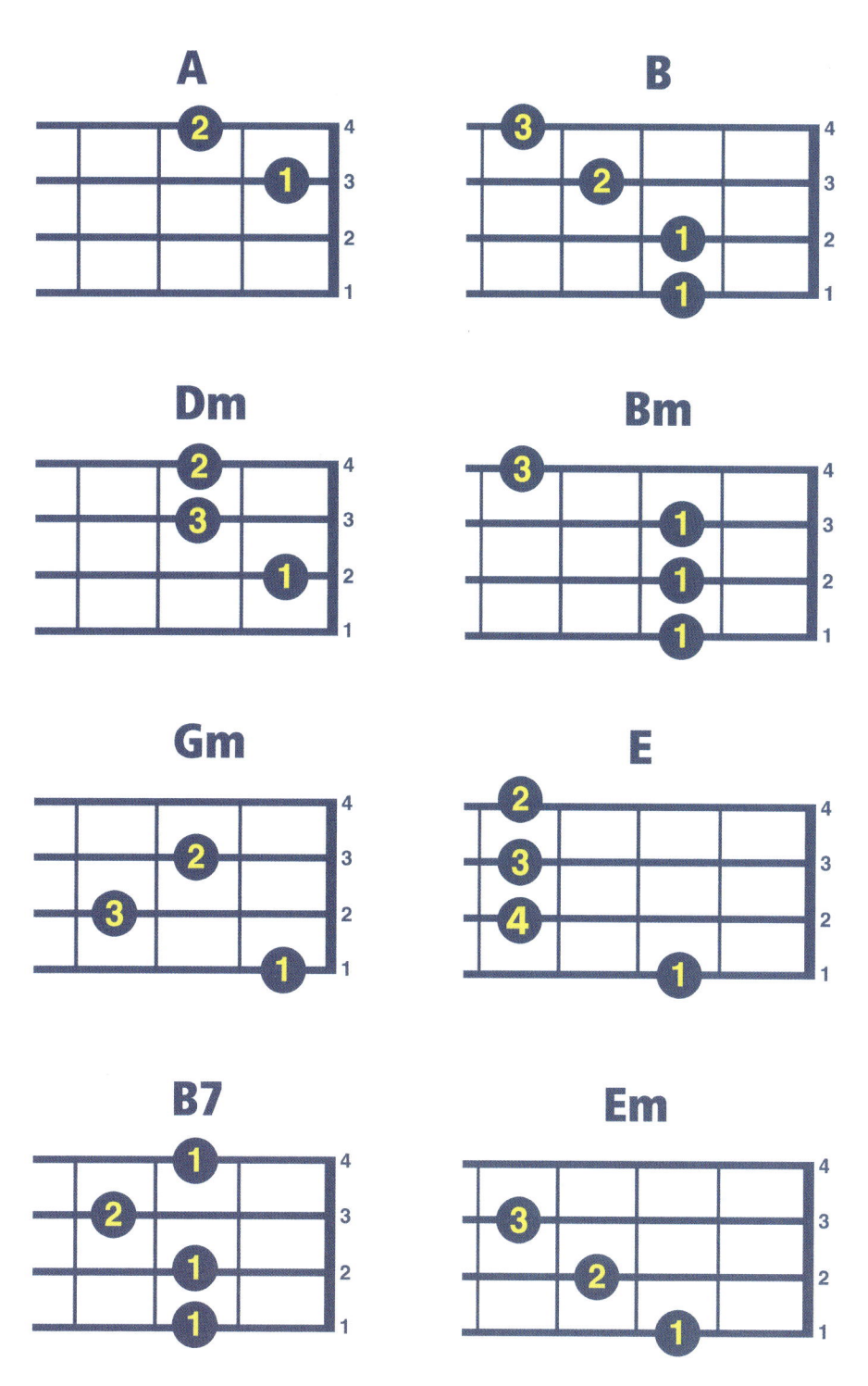

EASY UKULELE

15. POP SONG EXAMPLES

The following are examples of chord progressions from well-known pop songs, with a recommended strumming pattern for each. If you're not familiar with any of these, be sure to look them up and give them a listen.

Remember to start slowly, with one strum per chord. Once you know the progression by heart, and have the tune clearly in your mind, try the suggested strumming pattern. I recommend strumming through the chords at least 20 times before trying to sing. Check out my **4 Essential Ukulele Strumming Patterns** YouTube video for some helpful demonstrations and exercises.

COUNTING STARS by OneRepublic

Am C G F

Strum four downs on each chord.

↓ ↓ ↓ ↓
1 2 3 4

LET IT BE by The Beatles

VERSE: C G Am F
C G F C

CHORUS: Am G F C
C G F C

↓   ↓
1 2 3 4

Strum two slow downs on each chord.

NO WOMAN NO CRY by Bob Marley

CHORUS: C G Am F
C F C G

VERSE: C G Am F

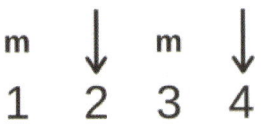

m ↓ m ↓
1 2 3 4

Play "mute strum mute strum" on each chord.

EASY UKULELE

The following three songs all use the same "mute strum mute strum" pattern, repeated twice per chord. Make sure to count a total of four "mute strums" per chord.

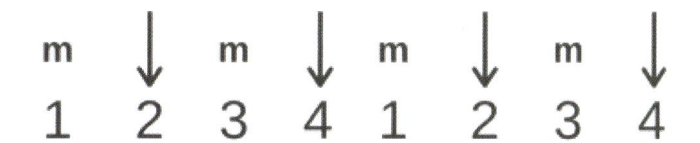

m ↓ m ↓ m ↓ m ↓
1 2 3 4 1 2 3 4

I'M YOURS *by Jason Mraz*

C   G   Am   F

DON'T WORRY BE HAPPY *by Bobby McFerrin*

G   Am   C   G

THREE LITTLE BIRDS *by Bob Marley*

CHORUS: A   A   D   A

VERSE: A   E   A   D
             A   E   D   A

See the **More Chords** section for the A and E chords and my **Easy E Chord** YouTube video for variations. Note the A is played twice at the beginning.

EASY UKULELE

LEAVING ON A JET PLANE *by John Denver*

G   C   G   C
G   C   D   D

↓   ↓↑   ↑↓↑
1   2   3 4

Strum "down, down up, up down up" on each chord. Note the D is played twice.

LOSING MY RELIGION *by R.E.M.*

Am   Em   Am   Em
Am   Em   Dm   G

Strum "down, down up, up down up" twice per chord. See the **More Chords** section for Em and Dm.

↓   ↓↑   ↑↓↑   ↓   ↓↑   ↑↓↑
1   2   3 4   1   2   3 4

RIPTIDE *by Vance Joy*

Am   G   C   C

Strum "down down, up down up" on each chord. Note the pause after the first two downs. Riptide is played pretty fast, but start slowly to get the chord transitions on time.

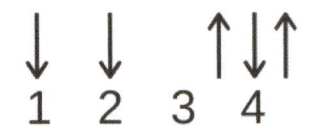

↓   ↓   ↑↓↑
1   2   3 4

PRACTICE MAKES PROGRESS

EASY UKULELE

Dear Musician,

Thank you so much for purchasing and playing through *Easy Ukulele*!

Have a favorite song to play? Why not make a quick video or audio recording and post it on social media, tagging Pierrehachemusic.com to share the joy of strumming and singing! And don't forget to subscribe to my YouTube Channel, **Pierre Hache Music!**

If you found this book to be a useful, fun and cost effective way to achieve your musical goals, please consider leaving a review on Amazon. Let's bring the **JOY** of strumming and singing into homes all over the world! Each review really helps with search rankings and sales, and I truly appreciate every single one.

Stay tuned for more videos, books and online courses!

Pierrehachemusic.com

Happy strumming!

Pierre